English for Communication

GW00505055

ENGLISH FOR COMMUNICATION

A. A. COLEBY

SECOND EDITION

John Murray Albemarle Street London

Contents

Introduction

The purpose of this book is to provide visual and factual material, the study and use of which will give a student constant practice in the handling of language for a specific purpose. The student or teacher who requires ideas to stimulate imaginative or creative writing, who wants help in grammatical analysis or the technical details of expression, who needs practice in 'literary' comprehension, definitions of shades of meaning, paraphrase, summary, correction of errors, ambiguities and faulty syntax, who wishes for rules for sentences or paragraph construction or for spelling lists and vocabulary improvement in the context of single sentences or 'through experience', will have to look elsewhere. This book provides something to say: it is up to the student guided by the teacher to say it in the clearest, most efficient manner possible. In each chapter, information of a practical, non-literary kind is provided and the two or three questions at the end demand close study and thorough absorption of this material and then a logical reorganization and presentation of it.

1 A Road Accident

In the diagram, *A* is a very large, slow-moving furniture remover's lorry travelling on the main road from Ludsby to Larchester. It is passing the road sign warning that the main road is joined by a minor road to the left from Deepdale, when the driver notices a fast sports car, *C*, emerge from the minor road and cross in front of him—with plenty of room to spare, considering that no traffic is coming from Larchester and the lorry is moving quite slowly. The sports car did not stop at the road junction, but was not compelled to do so, since it had passed only a 'Give Way' sign. Unfortunately, the driver of a saloon car, *B*, which is overtaking the lorry, has his vision of the warning sign and the road entrance obscured by the lorry, although he can see that no traffic is approaching from Larchester. When the sports car suddenly appears in front of him, he is unable to avoid a collision. Neither road is subjected to a speed limit. *A* is travelling at 30 mph, *B* at 60 mph and *C* at 25 mph when the collision occurs.

1 Write the statements that each of the three drivers might give to the police.

2 Imagine that the drivers of both cars are being prosecuted for driving without due care and attention. Make out a case in defence of each driver to be addressed to the magistrate (address him as 'Sir').

You may invent details concerning the drivers' temperaments and visibility and road and weather conditions, though you must be reasonably consistent.

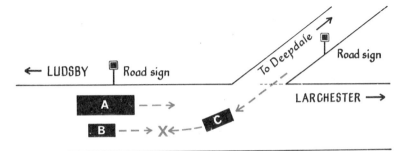

2 Leisure Time

A new town, Ludsby, is to be built in the Midlands to absorb an 'overspill' population of about 50 000 from London. The planning committee for this new town is prepared to pay for two entertainment projects to be built in the town centre, and will consider any two of the following: a swimming pool; a disco; a bingo hall; a cinema; a bowling alley.

Imagine that you are the newly appointed Planning Officer for Ludsby. The Planning Committee of a nearby town of similar population has had experience of building and operating all the projects to be considered, and the Planning Officer of that town has sent you a list of the building costs and the net annual profit received from them (lines 1 and 2 of the table· opposite). He has also sent you figures showing the average weekly attendance at each entertainment project for the age group 15 to 25 (line 3), for the age group 25 to 50 (line 4), and for those people above 50 (line 5).

You have also been informed that young married couples with

small children will constitute most of the population of the new town, that a substantial part will comprise middle-aged parents with teenage children, and that there will be very few elderly residents.

FIGURES FROM NEIGHBOURING TOWN'S PLANNING OFFICER

	Pool	Disco	Bingo	Cinema	Bowling alley
Building cost	£500 000	£150 000	£200 000	£300 000	£600 000
Annual profit	£10 000 (LOSS)	£15 000	£70 000	£10 000	£3 000
Weekly attendance 15–25	400	2 000	50	500	350
Weekly attendance 25–50	200	50	1 000	350	200
Weekly attendance over 50	50	—	3 000	100	—

Write a report for the Planning Committee, summarizing the information given by these sets of figures and recommending the two projects that you think would serve the new community best. Give reasons for supporting your two chosen projects. These reasons need not be entirely financial; they must bear in mind the kind of population of which the new town will be composed, and can be concerned with considerations of the health, educational and social needs of that population.

3 Moving

At the moment you live with your wife, your teenage daughter, Anne, and your eight-year-old son, Mark, in a rented house in a village six miles outside a large industrial town, Newham, where you work in a textile factory. You pay £23 per week rent for the house, which is large and semi-detached.

Your mother writes to you offering to let you and your family live in a terraced house which she owns near the centre of Newham for £12 per week rent. It is smaller than the one you occupy at present but in addition to the lower rent another big advantage as far as you are concerned is that you would save the £8 per week you at present pay on bus fares travelling to and from work and for entertainment at weekends. Your family is discussing the matter one evening.

'I don't much fancy a smaller, darker house,' says your wife, 'but I would be much nearer the supermarkets, which are much cheaper than the shops here. I'm not sure that it would be good for Mark to change schools at the moment, though. The house would probably get dirtier in town and would take more cleaning.'

'I won't be able to help Farmer Dawes with his cows if we move,' says Mark, 'and there's only the streets to play in at Newham. I've plenty of fields and meadows round here.'

'And I suppose I would have to give up my riding lessons with Farmer Dawes,' interrupts Anne, 'and I've so many friends in the village. But I wouldn't have to get the bus to work every day, and again every Friday to the disco.'

Write a letter to your mother accepting or rejecting her offer, giving your reasons and stating all the different aspects of the situation you had to bear in mind before making your decision. Express gratitude for her offer, and, whatever your decision, make the tone appropriately informal.

4 Retailing

You are to become the manager of a village shop. You study the books of the previous manager, and the table below shows your analysis of the average net profit per day for each particular commodity, showing the selling trends of each, in the first column six years ago, in the second column three years ago, and in the third column for last year.

The village is six miles from a fairly large town, but the bus service is poor and there is no railway station. It therefore tends to be a 'dormitory village', and the customers of the shop are children from the local schools and housewives of all ages, most of whose husbands work in the town. A new estate of privately owned houses, which is expected to be occupied largely by newly married couples, is just being erected, and there are plans for the building of a small supermarket nearby. Many old-age pensioners use the shop, but they constitute only a small part of the total custom.

Write a letter to the area manager of your chain of shops explaining your analysis, indicating the trends and the implications of them, and saying what changes in selling lines you propose, and why.

Commodity	Average profit per day six years ago	Three years ago	Last year
Bread	£2·10	£2·30	£4·00
Milk	£1·70	£2·40	£3·50
Chocolate sweets	£1·10	£1·50	£2·50
Boiled sweets	40p	30p	30p
Frozen food	£3·20	£4·10	£6·50
Cigarettes	£1·20	£1·20	£1·50
Flour	35p	30p	50p
Fresh vegetables	90p	70p	£1·20
Tinned pet food	£1·50	£2·30	£3·40
Deodorants	60p	90p	£1·20
Wine	£2·10	£3·10	£7·20
Patent medicines	18p	20p	40p
Razor blades	17p	15p	20p

5 Four Witnesses

At a local club, a young girl, Shirley, has collapsed and has had to be taken to hospital as a result of taking a dangerous combination of illegal drugs. You are a detective whose special task is to investigate cases concerning the possession of such drugs, and there have been more than a few instances of this kind of incident in your town recently. You are very anxious to trace the source of the drugs, or at least to find out more about the problem, possibly even to get enough evidence to enable you to apply for a search warrant. You have questioned four people who were in the club at the time, and the questions were more or less identical because you were looking for the kind of contradictory statement which might indicate guilt and enable you to pursue your enquiries more intensely in one direction. This is your notebook summary of the evidence supplied by each of the four witnesses:

John (a rich young man of twenty-five: a sports-car enthusiast):
'I was not talking to Shirley at the time, but I knew she was mixing in my group because I heard her laugh once or twice and you could always pick her out by her high-pitched laugh. I know most of the girls who come here. Shirley was quite popular, though she had only been coming a few weeks. The time was about 9.30. I remember "Ride to Heaven" had just finished playing. I hadn't noticed Shirley drinking much earlier in the evening, though I did not take much notice. I had seen her dancing once, but then again she might have been dancing much more for all I know.'

Jean (a close friend of Shirley's):
'This is all most upsetting. I didn't know Shirley took drugs. We had not been coming here long, but thought it was a nice club. Shirley was certainly happy here, always laughing and joking, and very popular. It would have been about half-past nine when she collapsed. There was no record playing at the time. Several people were near her at the time, but I was nearest and was not aware that anything unusual was happening or that she felt ill. We had had a few dances, but not many because we especially wanted to talk to this group of people.'

6

Harry (he serves at the bar):

'The time was exactly 9.30. I am certain of that because another helper arrives then as it is about our busiest time. "Ride to Heaven" had just been playing. I had served Shirley and her friends with one or two drinks during the evening, but not many really. She was with quite a large group and they were at the other end of the bar from where I was serving. I don't think she had danced much. She wasn't much of a dancer really—in fact, not the sort of girl you'd notice much at all, though she mixed well. I thought she turned a bit pale towards 9.30. I think that sports-car crowd she's been going with for the few weeks she's been coming are up to no good.'

Jim (a member of the group with whom Shirley had talked most of the evening):

'What a thing to happen to Shirley. She hadn't been coming long but she was a very nice girl: I'd given her two or three rides in my sports car. She always seemed to cheer people up, mainly because of that happy, infectious laugh she had. You could hear it all round the club, even when the record player was on—and that "Ride to Heaven" gets on my nerves. Yes, I suppose it was about half-past nine. Shirley had been laughing and talking most of the evening, but did not drink much and was not a great dancer.'

One of these witnesses has clearly invited suspicion. Write a brief report to your superior officer explaining why, and saying that you feel strongly enough to want to search or question him or her more closely.

6 The Twins' Playroom

On the opposite page is a plan of Mr and Mrs Smith's bungalow, where they live with their two-year-old twins and Mr Smith's aged father, who likes peace and quiet and dislikes the noise made by the twins. Mr and Mrs Smith have decided to have a playroom with immediate access through french windows to the garden built on one side of the bungalow. The question is, which side? Mrs Smith spends almost all her time in the lounge or kitchen and wants to keep an eye on the twins. She also wants them to be in a position to get as much sunshine as possible. There is no room for an extension taking up part of the drive. The lounge has a corner window which the Smiths want to preserve at all costs. The main road carries a lot of heavy traffic and is separated from the garden by only a scanty hedge. And, of course, the playroom must be kept as far away from Mr Smith's father as possible. There is, therefore, no ideal solution and the Smiths have referred the matter to their architect and have asked for his advice.

Put yourself in the architect's place and write a reply, listing alternative positions for the playroom and suggesting advantages and disadvantages to each.

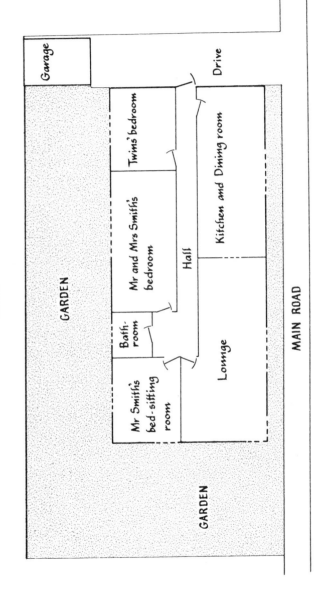

South

Garage

GARDEN

Mr Smith's bed-sitting room

Bath-room

Mr and Mrs Smith's bedroom

Twins' bedroom

Hall

Lounge

Kitchen and Dining room

Drive

GARDEN

MAIN ROAD

9

7 Selling Petrol

The selling of petrol is a fiercely competitive business for roadside service stations that offer no other service facilities. Sales are therefore promoted by offering various extra attractions to the customer, such as the giving away of drinking glasses for a number of vouchers which will have to be saved over three or four visits; the giving away of souvenir photographs of pop stars and footballers; the selling of other produce such as potatoes in quantities so large as to be inconvenient for retail shops, but which can be easily carried by car and bought cheaply; the occasional or permanent reduction of prices; the giving of well-known trading stamps at so many per gallon; the provision of special services for mopeds and some motor-

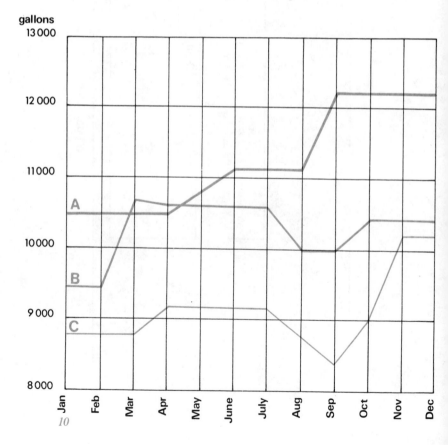

cycles which run on a mixture of petrol and oil; the employment of glamorous attendants.

Imagine that you are the area manager of a company controlling three service stations, A, B and C, which in January of the year in question offer none of the above attractions.

The stations are situated on main roads in the countryside, each with a comparable flow of traffic. At various times during the year each station adopts one or more of the promotional gimmicks and the effects on their sales are shown in the graph opposite. The list below shows what new steps were taken during each month of the year.

February	Station B begins giving trading stamps.
March	Station C gives away pictures of pop stars and footballers with every four gallons bought.
April	Station B gives free drinking glasses for 16 vouchers, one voucher being given for every two gallons bought. Station A gives pictures of pop stars and footballers.
May	Station A sells large bags of potatoes and cartons of eggs more cheaply than they can be bought at supermarkets—provided that the customer buys at least two gallons of petrol. Station C starts giving glasses on the same terms as Station B.
June	Station A reduces the price of all grades by 1p per gallon. All three stations install two-stroke mixture pumps for mopeds and small motorcycles.
July	Station B stops giving trading stamps and reduces prices of all grades by 1p per gallon. Station C stops giving away pictures, and starts selling potatoes and eggs like Station A. Station A gives drinking glasses.
August	Station A starts giving trading stamps.
September	Stations B and C employ glamorous girl attendants.
October	Station C starts giving trading stamps. Stations A and B install a cheap car-washing service.

Write a report to the national sales manager of your company, giving details of the situation of each station and each sales promotion that was tried. State clearly which promotions were, in your opinion, successful, and which were unsuccessful, and in each case suggest a reason. The tone and style of the report, of course, must be formal.

8 Besieged

A man has escaped from prison, stolen a shotgun and, having been cornered by the police, is now holding a woman and small child hostage in farmhouse *A* in the plan opposite. There is another farmhouse at *B* and other features which might influence the situation are indicated in the plan. The police have paused to assess the situation and have temporarily encamped at the cross behind *B*. The police have been in communication with the man by means of the telephone in the farmhouse, and he is demanding that the police provide him with a car and allow him to drive away without following; otherwise, he has threatened to harm or even kill the hostages. There are five courses of action open to the police:

1 to comply with his request for a car and to hope that he will then subsequently release the hostages unharmed;
2 to shoot teargas into the farmhouse—this will painfully afflict the eyes, lungs and nasal passages of all the occupants, though it might persuade the man to yield the hostages;
3 to send into the farmhouse a dog which could be made to discriminate between the three occupants by being conditioned to the man's scent;
4 to carry fire-arms and approach the farmhouse directly or indirectly from one or more sides of the house, hoping to surprise, shoot or overpower the man;
5 to refuse to comply with any request he might make, and, whilst taking no offensive action, simply to wait and watch until eventually hunger, weakness, discomfort and tiredness force him to release the hostages and then surrender.

As the police officer responsible for apprehending the man, send back a report on the situation to your superintendent, outline the advantages and disadvantages of each possible course of action, and state with reasons what you propose to do. You know that there is enough food and water in the house for three or four days, but you are very anxious about the safety of the hostages because the criminal is known to be mentally unstable.

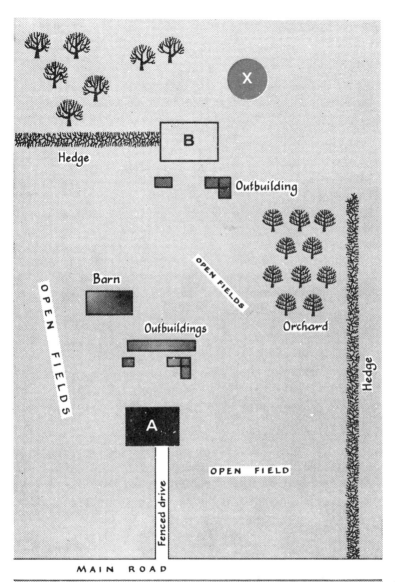

9 Crossroads

Opposite is a map showing a large roundabout on the outskirts of Caenthorpe, a large industrial town. The roundabout is situated at the junction of Grebe Avenue and Banks Road with the main road from Caenthorpe to Marlton.

The roundabout has a tall iron railing round it specifically so that pedestrians may not cross the road at the roundabout and use it as a refuge. There are not, however, any railings at the edge of any of the pavements.

On the northern side of Grebe Avenue are a few much-used shops: a Post Office, a greengrocer's, a newsagent's, and a general store which stocks a very wide range of items, from fruit and vegetables to general groceries, children's toys, and hardware. For the general use of all shoppers, a large car park is situated behind the Post Office and adjoining the premises of a Public House; the entrance to it is on the northern side of the Public House.

About four hundred yards from the junction, a secondary school is situated to the south of Grebe Avenue. Apart from this and the shops, the Avenue is fronted by rows of houses on both sides, and housing estates lie to the north and south, the one to the north including a residential centre for elderly people. Houses also face the south-west corner of the roundabout and both sides of the main road south of the roundabout.

A supermarket faces the south-east corner of the roundabout, and a branch library the north-east corner. Housing estates are situated to the north and south of Banks Road.

At the spot A, to the south-west of the roundabout, is a bus stop which is also the terminus of a busy route. The bus, therefore, often stands there for ten minutes or more before returning to the centre of Caenthorpe. This has happened for many years, but recently a few pedestrians have been knocked down, as they made their way from the bus across Grebe Avenue towards the Post Office, by cars coming mostly from the Caenthorpe direction which were blocked from view by the stationary bus.

The police have therefore decided that the bus terminus must be moved to one of the other three corners of the roundabout. Each corner has a straight pavement of adequate length, though the supermarket manager has written to the police pointing out that his corner is a little longer and wider than the others. The bus is not allowed to stand in the main road because of the volume of traffic, and Grebe Avenue and Banks Road are too narrow for the bus to use in turning.

There is much more traffic, including heavy lorries, using the main road than either of the other two. The arrows on the plan show the directions of traffic flow. Any vehicles turning right at the round-about would not have their vision as much obscured by the bus as would those turning left. Most of the Grebe Avenue and Banks Road traffic goes to and from Caenthorpe town centre.

The bus service is used by the pupils of the school, the residents of all the housing estates, and the customers of the library, the public house and all the shops.

You are a police officer whose job it is to decide at which corner to site the bus stop. Write a report to your senior officer (simply address him as 'Sir') stating:

1 your chosen site;
2 the advantages and disadvantages of your chosen site;
3 the advantages and disadvantages of the two sites you have rejected.

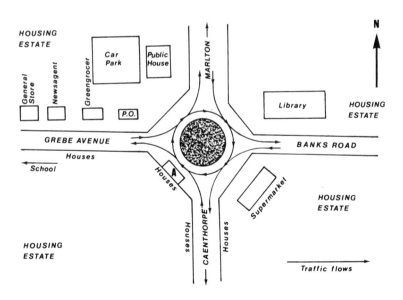

10 Traffic Problem

Opposite we have a plan of a town centre. The road leading past the Town Hall, Central Parade, is to be closed all Saturday afternoon because of a civic function. The main shopping streets of the town are Kent Street, Bridge Street, Austin Road and Central Avenue. Arrows indicate one-way streets and bus routes. Also marked are a cinema, a school, a football stadium at which there is an important match, and a church in which a wedding is scheduled to take place. West Road carries the heaviest traffic, some of it bound for the football stadium and some for London Road, an arterial road leading out of town.

1 You are asked to re-route a bus service which normally passes along West Avenue, Central Parade and London Road, and another service passing in the opposite direction, along London Road, Central Parade and West Avenue. The two services do not have to follow the same diversionary route. There is no ideal solution. Point out the advantages and disadvantages of the route you choose.

2 You are asked to direct a motorist from the cinema to the football stadium.

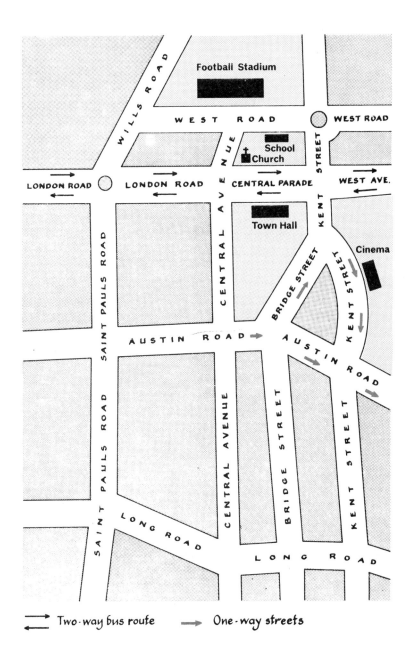

Football Stadium

WILLS ROAD

WEST ROAD

WEST ROAD

School

Church

CENTRAL AVENUE

LONDON ROAD

LONDON ROAD

CENTRAL PARADE

WEST AVE.

KENT STREET

Town Hall

Cinema

SAINT PAULS ROAD

BRIDGE STREET

KENT STREET

AUSTIN ROAD

AUSTIN ROAD

SAINT PAULS ROAD

LONG ROAD

CENTRAL AVENUE

BRIDGE STREET

KENT STREET

LONG ROAD

Two-way bus route ⟶ One-way streets

17

11 A Legal Problem

The manager of a supermarket has collected together several eye-witness accounts of an incident that occurred at the entrance to his store and this appears to be a true, unbiassed account of the sequence of events:

As Mr Green was shopping in the supermarket, he picked up and examined many children's toys, but decided to buy only one of them and replaced the rest on the shelves. At the cash desk, he paid for the one toy and several articles of food, which he then placed in his shopping bag, and walked through the entrance door of the store. A store assistant, Mr Jones, had been watching Mr Green's examination of several toys and thought he had placed one into his shopping bag and one into his wire basket, so that as he walked out he had two toys in the shopping bag. Mr Jones therefore followed him, and as he reached him on the pavement outside the store he attempted to arrest him and told him to accompany him to the manager's office, as he had reason to believe that he had in his bag more goods than he had purchased. Mr Green refused, saying that he had in his bag only what he had paid for. Mr Jones then insisted that he come inside the store, and placed his hand on Mr Green's arm. Mr Green became angry, and punched Mr Jones hard in the face, causing him to reel backwards. At this point a passing constable intervened and then took statements from all concerned.

An examination by the constable of the shopping bag showed that Mr Green had only one toy and thus had not stolen anything. Mr Green is charging Mr Jones with wrongful arrest and battery, while Mr Jones is accusing Mr Green of battery, and Mr Green claims that he acted in self-defence.

Imagine that you are a solicitor to whom the manager has sent this account of what happened so that you may advise him of which charges are likely to succeed in court, for he is thinking of offering Mr Green compensation so that the matter does not reach the courts.

The relevant sections of your law books give the following information (the plaintiff is the person making the accusation, the defendant is the accused person, and 'felony' means a crime):

Battery

Battery is any act of the defendant which directly causes some physical contact with the person of the plaintiff without the plaintiff's consent. There is no battery unless there is an act by the defendant. Merely to obstruct is not of itself enough.

Self-defence

If Mr Green hits Mr Jones or damages his clothes, then he commits a trespass to the person or to goods. If Mr Green should prove that he did so to defend himself against Mr Jones he may have the justification of self-defence to an action in battery or trespass to goods brought against him by Mr Jones. The defendant must prove that in the circumstances it was reasonable that he should defend himself and that the force used by him was reasonable. One may in this way resist an unlawful arrest. In considering what is reasonable force, it will be material to consider whether the plaintiff could have escaped, or whether he resisted with the most reasonable means available.

Arrest

1 By a policeman with a warrant:
 A policeman who arrests a person under a warrant performs a lawful act.

2 Without a warrant:
 A private person who has reasonable cause to believe that a particular person has committed a felony may justifiably arrest him if that felony has in fact been committed. The same rule does not apply to a constable, for a constable is justified in arresting a person without warrant upon reasonable suspicion of a felony having been committed, and of the person being guilty of it.

Write a letter to the manager advising him whether each charge is likely to be successful or unsuccessful in court, and giving your opinion of Mr Green's claim of acting in self-defence. Show the reasons for each of your conclusions.

12 The 'Blind Spot'

●   ●

You will almost certainly have done this before. The two large dots at the top of this passage are two inches apart. Close your left eye and keep your right eye focused on the left dot. Move the page towards your face and you will find that, at a point about four inches in front of your eyes, the right dot momentarily disappears from view. You can repeat the process by closing the right eye and looking at the right dot with the left eye. Below is a very much simplified diagram of an eyeball showing how rays of light travel from an object through the lens of the eye to the sensitive back lining of the eye, the retina, and the image they form is then conducted via the optic nerve to the brain. The retina is not sensitive at the point where the optic nerve leaves the eyeball.

Now explain clearly why each of the dots disappears as described above.

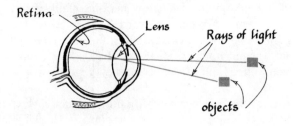

13 Sell a Car

In a showroom are four new cars, the main features of which are indicated in the table below. Car A is a sports car with sleek lines, fast acceleration and many fitted extras such as a radio, oil pressure gauge, rev. counter and cigarette lighter included in the price. Car B is a small and economical family man's car with limited head and leg room for passengers and a very small boot, but which has a reputation for being a reliable car. Cars C and D are also family saloons but have much more passenger and luggage space than Car B. Car C is the bigger one, and has many luxury features such as power-assisted steering and very fashionable upholstery. It also has the extras which are fitted to Car A. Car D has none of these special features and is more utilitarian in every respect, but is not as small as B and has a reputation for being just as reliable.

The country of manufacture is a consideration for the buyer of a car in that generally spare parts and service are more expensive for a foreign car than for a British one.

	A	B	C	D
Price	10 000	3 500	£7 000	£5 000
No. of passengers	2	3	4	4
Miles per gallon	23	45	30	36
Maximum speed (mph)	120	75	110	90
Second-hand value after two years	£7 500	£2 300	£5 000	£2 500
Second-hand value after five years	£3 500	£1 500	£3 000	£1 600
Country of manfacture	Germany	France	Sweden	Britain

Imagine that you are a car salesman and are approached by a customer in his forties who, you would guess, has an average income and is almost certainly a family man. He tells you that he wishes to buy a new car. Decide which of the four you think will suit him best, and write an account of what you would say to him, comparing your chosen car favourably with the others.

14 Situations Vacant

The table below is a summary of information about each of the six 16 year-old school leavers named at the top of the six columns. It has been completed from confidential forms sent by the careers teachers of the six pupils to you, a careers officer. In the Appearance, Speech and Reliability sections, A is excellent, B is well above average and quite impressive, C is average for a 16 year-old, D is below average and E is very poor indeed. In the subject sections, A means very good with a very high grade expected in G.C.E. examinations, B means good with reasonable grades expected in G.C.E. examinations, C means of average ability with good C.S.E. grades expected, D is below average and E is very poor. In the Personality section, A is very assertive socially and a confident and impressive personality, B is moderately sociable and assertive, C is steady and sensible and by no means shy or nervous, D is quiet and a little hesitant and nervous, and E is very shy and retiring.

	Peter Jones	Chris Cook	John Bell	Mary Johnson	Jane Green	Judith Miles
Appearance	A	B	C	A	B	C
Personality	B	C	D	A	B	C
Speech	B	C	D	B	B	D
Reliability	B	B	B	B	B	B
English	C	C	C	C	A	C
Maths	C	C	A	C	C	D
Science subjects	D	C	B	C	C	D
Woodwork/Metalwork	D	B	C			
Needlework/Homecraft				D	D	A
Commercial Subjects				C	A	D
Art	C	D	E	D	E	C

Imagine that you are a Careers officer, and for any *one* of the pupils listed in the table, choose what you think is the most suitable job for him or her from the list of vacancies below and then write a letter of introduction for him or her to the employer who is offering the job. The examination grades mentioned above are only what are expected, because your letter must be dated July and so the results have not yet been published. Because the forms sent to you were confidential, you cannot simply reproduce the information as it is in the table, but you must describe your chosen candidate's personal qualities and academic and practical ability in general terms appropriate to the selected job. Remember also that it is your purpose to help them get the job.

List of vacancies:

1 Accountant, to deal with costing, year-end accounts, credit control and cash flow procedures. Apply to the Personnel Officer, British Tissues Ltd.

2 Telephonist/Receptionist who must enjoy meeting people. Duties will include: telephone work, customer liaison, making appointments etc. Apply to the Manager, Craven's Printing Co. Ltd.

3 Young man required to train as a salesman in the motor trade. No experience necessary as full training will be given. He should be smart, intelligent and willing to learn. Apply to the Manager, George Holmes Engineering Co. Ltd.

4 Trainee draughtsman required for a light engineering company. Opportunity for further study to become a fully qualified design engineer. Apply to the Personnel Manager, Thos. Ward Ltd.

5 Cook wanted for a small private hotel. Opportunity to train under an experienced chef. Apply to the Castle Hotel.

6 Secretary/Shorthand Typist needed by City Centre Solicitors. Interesting, varied work and good rate of pay. Apply to Clarke and Buxton.

15 Security

As the night security officer of a stately home, it is your responsibility to ensure that the wing of the house shown in the diagram has the best defence available in the circumstances to minimize the possibility of the theft of any of the equally valuable paintings hung in each of the four rooms, *A, B, C, D*. The dotted lines represent windows and the other gaps are doors: all are numbered for easy reference. *E* is a door on the corridor leading to this wing which cannot be locked or fitted with a burglar alarm, but can be closed.

Absolute security is impossible because the owner of the house will provide you with only two locks for the doors, one burglar alarm and a dog. The windows are particularly vulnerable and it is advisable that the dog, which can be left to roam at will anywhere in the wing, has easy access to all of them. The door at which the burglar alarm is fitted must be closed or the dog will trigger the alarm.

State how you would allocate your alarm and two locks and how you would use the dog, explaining what would be the advantages of your method of allocation and the disadvantages of any alternative method.

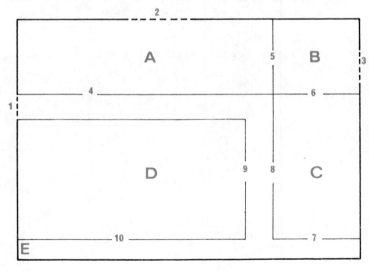

16 Travelling to Work

Mr Smith has got a new job which is fifteen miles away from his home and he has to decide whether it will be better to go to and from work each day in the firm's bus or to drive his own car. He has jotted down a few notes which give the facts relevant to the situation in order to help him make up his mind. They are as follows:

Return bus fare £1·80 a day—petrol £1·80 a gallon—car does thirty miles to the gallon—wear and tear on car using it every day—tyres £40 a year—maintenance £150 a year—tax £80 a year—comprehensive insurance £80 a year—I would tax and maintain the car even if I did not use it for work—car would depreciate even if not used—easier and more relaxing by bus—meet other people from the firm—bus takes ten minutes longer than the car for the journey—ten minutes to walk to where the bus picks me up—sometimes could go shopping on the way home with my own car.

Make Mr Smith's decision, and write down what you think would be his explanation to his wife of that decision.

17 Personalities

Jean is a nurse who has been sent for a year's training to a hospital abroad. The staff and patients are mostly elderly and she is feeling lonely. She therefore writes to a girl friend Judith, who lives in her home town, and asks for the names and addresses of any unattached boys she knows to whom she might write. Judith sends a list of three with the following information:

Jack is a sports-loving, outdoor type who plays in the local rugby team and frequents his local public house but also attends church regularly.

Ron is much more studious, spending his evenings at the local technical college, studying to pass exams to gain promotion at the bank where he works. For relaxation, he visits the theatre or cinema.

Mike likes folk singing, sports cars, dancing, and is a star player at the local tennis club. He is a teacher, and can be very serious and strong-minded about the values and principles he believes in, though these are not religious.

Jean herself is a quiet, thoughtful, reflective sort of girl, who reads a lot but also has a passion for dancing when she gets the opportunity. She is not interested in or good at any sport, but likes walking in the countryside and studying wildlife. She is also deeply religious. Her interests do not correspond to those of any of the three boys, but she decides to write to one of them.

Either   If you are a girl, put yourself in Jean's position, and compose the letter.

or   If you are a boy, imagine that you have received an introductory and explanatory letter from Jean, put yourself in the position of one of the boys, and compose a reply. Whatever your reaction, the tone must be polite and reasonably friendly.

18 The House that Jack Wants

Jack is a young man about to get married and is looking for a house. He is offered a house to rent at £25 per week which includes the payment of rates. It is in the town centre, and so is near his job and the shops. He also knows of a house he likes which is for sale at £20 000 and is on the outskirts of the town. He has saved enough money to pay a deposit of £2 000 on this house, and after discussing the possibility of a loan with a Building Society, he learns that after paying his deposit he must repay the loan at the rate of £150 per month for twenty-five years. The Building Society estimates that the value of the house will increase at an average rate of £800 per year. The rates payable on the house are £210 per year.

Imagine that you are Jack's uncle, that he has asked your advice about which of these offers to accept, and write a letter in reply. Try to point out advantages for each possible course of action, but finally recommend one of them to Jack. Bear in mind such considerations as the fact that the house Jack is buying will be his own in twenty-five years' time, the cost of decoration, repairs and insurance, and Jack's desire to save as much money as he can in the next few years.

19 Select a Football Team

Brocklehurst

Williams   Jackson   Bentley

Smith   Parsons   Stanland

Gray   Cheetham   Morrison   Fox

Reserves: Hill (*attacker*), Peck and Metcalfe (*defenders*).

You are the manager of a football team which is on tour. Illness and injuries have reduced the number of fit players in your party to fourteen. These are: Brocklehurst, who is now your only recognized goalkeeper. Williams, Jackson and Bentley are your back line of defence, and of these, Jackson cannot play effectively anywhere other than in the centre of the field, whereas Williams and Bentley are strong, speedy backs who frequently make attacking raids down the wings, Williams on the right and Bentley on the left. Smith, Parsons and Stanland are the mid-field players, Parsons preferring to play only in the centre and Stanland on the left, though Smith is a good, versatile player, attacking and defending with equal power and vigour. Gray, Cheetham, Morrison and Fox constitute your forward line. Gray and Fox are the wingers, Gray usually occupying the right flank and Fox the left, though both can play on either side of the field, are fast and versatile and often drop back to assist the defence. Cheetham and Morrison are essentially goal-getters, fast, nimble opportunists, but highly specialized players who dislike playing in any other position. Your reserves have been Hill, a versatile attacker, Metcalfe, an all-round defender, and Peck, who is a safe defender but incapable of attacking with much effectiveness.

Now your problems are added to by the fact that in the last match Stanland and Fox were injured and you will have to play two of your reserves in the next match. You also know that your opponents for the next match are very strong in attack.

As the manager, decide which two of the reserves you will select, and then explain to Jackson, the captain, the reasons for your selection and what the tactical consequences will be.

20 Heating a Room

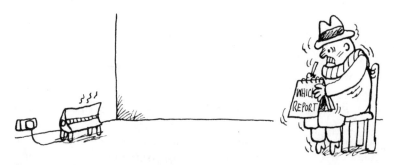

The diagrams opposite show the different performances of three radiant electric fires, *A, B* and *C,* in heating rooms of the same size. A coloured square shows the portion of the room which was comfortable after the fire had been switched on for one hour, and a coloured circle shows the portion of the room which was nearly comfortable after heating for one hour. A black shaded square shows an area comfortable after three hours' heating, and a black shaded circle the area nearly comfortable after three hours. A coloured circle in a black shaded square shows an area which was nearly comfortable after one hour and comfortable after three hours.

In every case the fire was in the same position, and the temperature outside the room was 40 °F (4·4 °C). Before an area could be considered 'comfortable' the air at 3 ft (0·9 metres) and 5 ft 6 in (1·65 metres) had to reach a temperature of 60 °F (15·6 °C). All the fires had an output of 3 kilowatts.

1 Describe and compare the performances of the different fires.

2 Say, giving your reasons, which fire you would choose to heat:
   (*a*) a lounge, the whole area of which will be used during an evening;
   (*b*) a dining room, used only at meal times, in which the dining table is situated in the centre of the room.

3 Explain the difference between 'radiant' and 'convected' and 'central' heating, and compare the advantages or disadvantages of each form.

Based on a report entitled 'Cheap, powerful electric radiant heaters' published in *Which?*, January 1965, by Consumers' Association, 14 Buckingham Street, London WC2.

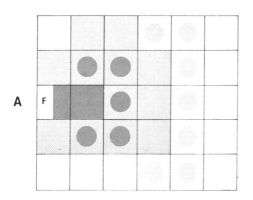

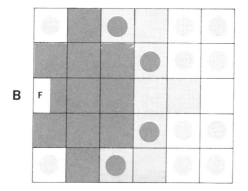

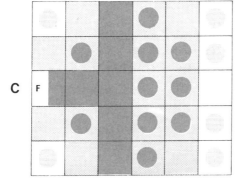

21 An Election

Below is a graph showing the changing fortunes of candidates *A* and *B* during a local election campaign. The figures on the left of the graph show the percentage of the electorate which supports each candidate; the percentage of uncommitted voters is also indicated.

Each candidate makes an election speech every other day and the changes in the voting intention as a result of the pledges and counter-attacks that they make are shown at two-day intervals, i.e. after each

Percentage of populace allegedly supporting each candidate and those uncommitted

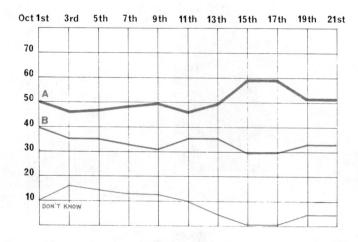

Oct.
1–3   *B* says he will introduce two Comprehensive schools in place of the present Grammar and Secondary Modern.
3–5   *B* proposes a re-planned shopping centre.
5–7   *A* points out that it will raise the rates.
7–9   *B* proposes a new by-pass; *A* calculates cost.
9–11   *B* proposes a new dance hall for youngsters.
11–13   *A* proposes a new factory employing 1000 unskilled women workers.
13–15   *A*'s party, in power in national Government, raises old-age pensions.
15–17   *A*'s party abolishes prescription charges.
17–19   There is a rise in the national rate of income tax.
19–21   A nationally known politician speaks in support of *B*.

has made one speech. The most important issues raised between these dates are given in the table. Because it is a local election, some of the issues are local ones, but each candidate is representative of a party which also constitutes part of the national Parliament, and A's party happens to be the one in power. The national fortunes of the parties therefore influence the electorate's opinion of their representative candidates and this shows strongly on the graph.

Imagine that you are to be an Independent candidate in this election and, by a careful study of the issues which concern the voters, arrive at some estimation of the kind of populace of which the ward is made up, and so write a speech making promises on the matters that you know influence their decisions and attacking your opponents on the basis of what you know their opinions are.

22 Food Values

It is common knowledge that the body requires three main types of food:

1 body-building food, or protein, which includes milk, cheese, eggs, meat, fish, peas, cereals and bread;
2 protective foods which are rich in vitamins and mineral salts and which help the body to resist ill-health: these include milk, cheese, butter, eggs, green vegetables, carrots, tomatoes and all kinds of fresh fruit;
3 energy-giving foods: this type could be of the class called carbohydrates, which have a high starch or sugar content and which include cereals, potatoes, honey and sugar; or fats, which include cream of milk, butter, cheese, beef fat, lard, oily fish such as herrings, and nut and vegetable oils such as margarine, and whose power of maintaining heat and activity in the body is two and a half times greater than that of starch.

Opposite is a chart showing the comparative average cost and amount of protein in seven foods. The price of potatoes, green vegetables and fruit, of course, is affected by many factors of supply and demand, but in general it may be stated that they are expensive by comparison with milk. Using as much information as you can gather from the chart, and as much of the above information as is relevant, *either* write an advertisement for milk which is persuasive mainly by being informative *or* write a lecture suitable for delivery to a group of schoolchildren and intended to persuade them of the financial advantages and nutritional value of milk.

Chart showing grammes of protein contained in specified portions of food

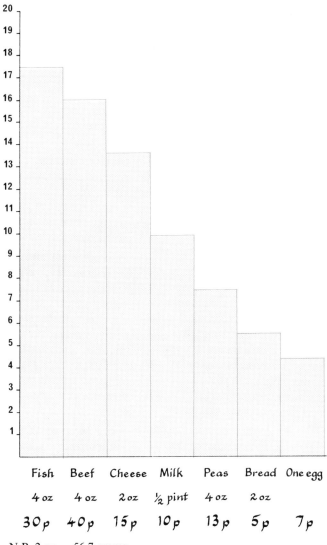

	Fish	Beef	Cheese	Milk	Peas	Bread	One egg
	4 oz	4 oz	2 oz	½ pint	4 oz	2 oz	
	30p	40p	15p	10p	13p	5p	7p

N.B. 2 oz = 56·7 grams
4 oz = 113·4 grams
1 loaf of bread = 800 grams = 28 oz = 37p = 2½p per oz

23 Cost and Sales

Opposite you see two graphs showing the relationship between the cost of a certain company's production of a pre-packed frozen food and the income from the sales. The sale is not subject to any seasonal variation and the cost of materials remains constant at £8 000 per month throughout the period under review, January 1973 to January 1977.

You can see from the graph that throughout 1973 and 1974 the company had only one way of trying to raise falling sales and that was by very expensive advertising campaigns. During the months these took place, of course, expenditure exceeded income, but sales always rose as a result. Very often the cause of a fall in sales was that the price of the product was increased in order to pay an extra wage demand. If such demands were not met and a strike ensued, as happened in July 1973, irreparable harm was done to the company because the loss of orders resulting from the failure of a regular supply was never fully recovered. When cost of production exceeded income from sales, however, as happened in October 1973 and April 1975, the company's only recourse was to reduce the labour force, i.e. make some workers redundant. The sales potential of the company was also influenced by the appearance of new firms packaging the same product and thus stealing part of the market. But in May 1975 and July 1976 new machines which enabled the firm to set in motion a new process were purchased and installed. The cost was high, but no higher than that of an advertising campaign. The result was that the product became cheaper because the cost of production fell owing to fewer workers being needed.

Imagine that you are appointed the General Manager of the firm in January 1977. You have been warned that a further wage demand is imminent, but the Board of Directors is willing to make £50 000 available for you to use as you wish. Decide whether you would pursue another advertising campaign or buy another new machine, and write a report for the next meeting of the Board explaining why you consider it wise to spend the money in this way.

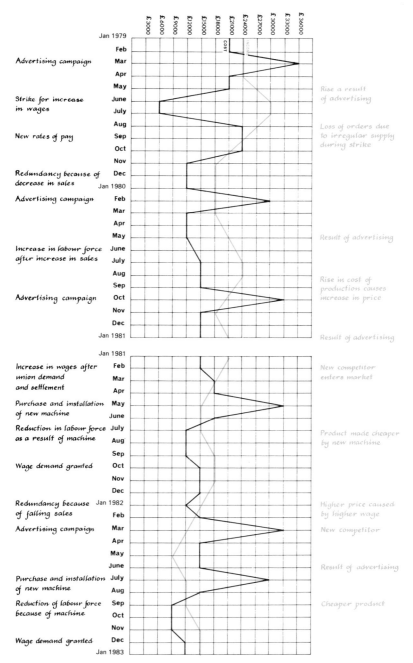

£3000 £6000 £9000 £12000 £15000 £18000 £21000 £24000 £27000 £30000 £33000 £36000

COST

Jan 1979
Feb
Advertising campaign — Mar
Apr
May — Rise a result of advertising
Strike for increase in wages — June / July
Aug — Loss of orders due to irregular supply during strike
New rates of pay — Sep
Oct
Nov
Redundancy because of decrease in sales — Dec / Jan 1980
Advertising campaign — Feb
Mar
Apr
May — Result of advertising
Increase in labour force after increase in sales — June / July
Aug — Rise in cost of production causes increase in price
Sep
Advertising campaign — Oct
Nov
Dec
Jan 1981 — Result of advertising

Jan 1981
Increase in wages after union demand and settlement — Feb / Mar / Apr — New competitor enters market
Purchase and installation of new machine — May / June
Reduction in labour force as a result of machine — July / Aug — Product made cheaper by new machine
Sep
Wage demand granted — Oct
Nov
Dec
Redundancy because of falling sales — Jan 1982 / Feb — Higher price caused by higher wage
Advertising campaign — Mar — New competitor
Apr
May
June — Result of advertising
Purchase and installation of new machine — July / Aug
Reduction of labour force because of machine — Sep / Oct — Cheaper product
Nov
Wage demand granted — Dec
Jan 1983

37

You receive a letter from a friend of yours who has been ejected from a political meeting. He was not actually arrested or charged but has been advised that his behaviour amounted to sedition, which is a common-law crime. He is inclined to become very excited by political questions, and voluble and aggressive in the expression of his opinions. Therefore, his ideas about freedom of speech and opinion have been outraged by this incident. At the same time, he was genuinely surprised by being told that his behaviour might well have been illegal, and, acknowledging you to be a more informed and better educated person than he is, writes this letter to ask for your advice:

Dear John,

I am enraged. I have just been thrown out of a meeting at the City Hall, and the steward accused me of seditious behaviour and said what I had done was a crime. I ask you! In this country that is supposed to be so democratic and you are supposed to be able to say what you like without fear of arrest! How can this be so? I want to know what you think, though, because I don't want to get arrested, not with a wife and children depending on me, and as you know I am always going along to meetings with my friends and we voice our opinions very loudly. On this particular night, we were shouting insults at that lout Smith and his gang who want to turn us into a totalitarian state and not let us voice our opinions. The nerve of the man, saying it is all for the good of the working classes. If his lot got into power, everyone would be a lot worse off than they are now. Surely we have a right to say so? What do you think? I think it's that lot who abuse free speech, taking advantage of the liberties we grant them in this country.

Yours,

Henry

Having received this letter, you go to the Library, consult books on law, and elicit the following information:

'Sedition is a common-law crime, which includes the doing of acts or the speaking of words with the intention of promoting feelings of ill-will or hostility between different classes of the Queen's subjects. If the words or acts (whatever the intention) have a direct tendency to cause unlawful meetings or disturbances, they are seditious, since a man is presumed to intend the natural consequences of his acts. This does not mean that there must be no full and free discussion, nor that there is any prohibition upon criticism, or even censure; but there must be no malignity, nor any imputation of corrupt or malicious motives, such as to incite people to take the law into their own hands and to provoke them to tumult and disorder.'

With this in mind, form your own opinion of Henry's behaviour, and write to him in a friendly manner, but making his position quite clear as regards the law, and offer him any advice you consider relevant.